DEEP SCARS

by Kaycie Davis

Order this book online at www.trafford.com
or email orders@trafford.com

Most Trafford titles are also available at major online book retailers.

© Copyright 2010 Kaycie Davis.
All rights reserved. No part of this publication may be reproduced, stored in a retrieval system, or transmitted, in any form or by any means, electronic, mechanical, photocopying, recording, or otherwise, without the written prior permission of the author.

Printed in Victoria, BC, Canada.

ISBN: 978-1-4269-2378-4 (sc)

Our mission is to efficiently provide the world's finest, most comprehensive book publishing service, enabling every author to experience success. To find out how to publish your book, your way, and have it available worldwide, visit us online at www.trafford.com

Trafford rev. 12/23/2009

 www.trafford.com

North America & international
toll-free: 1 888 232 4444 (USA & Canada)
phone: 250 383 6864 ♦ fax: 812 355 4082

This is an autobiography of the life of
Kaycie Davis

This is her story of domestic violence and abuse and is
dedicated to everyone who has suffered pain
and abuse from the person they love.

CONTENTS

Chapter 1	My Childhood	1
Chapter 2	My Accident	5
Chapter 3	Thee Loss of My Father	9
Chapter 4	Running Away	11
Chapter 5	The Visions	13
Chapter 6	Divorcing John	15
Chapter 7	My Trip to Colorado	17
Chapter 8	Meeting Paul	19
Chapter 9	Over the Bridge	21
Chapter 10	The Ax Handle	23
Chapter 11	Smashing Up the Van	27
Chapter 12	Paul's Parent's Visit	31
Chapter 13	My Legs Collapse	35
Chapter 14	Hurricane Diana	37
Chapter 15	Trying Again	39
Chapter 16	Paul Has a Close Call	43
Chapter 17	More Abuse	47
Chapter 18	The Burning	51
Chapter 19	The Shooting	55

Chapter 1
MY CHILDHOOD

I was born in Glen Cove, New York, on July 11, 1958. My family moved to Smithtown, NY, when I was four years old. That's when I began to realize something was different about my family.

My father was a construction worker who left in the mornings to go to work, while my mother would stay home to watch me. My sister, Terri, is my half sister and is seven years older than me, went to school.

Everything seemed to be fine while mother and I were home together until the afternoon. That was when she started drinking her screwdrivers. At that time, I didn't understand why mother's mood would change after several of these drinks.

Terri would come home from school, say hello to mother and I, and then she would go straight to her room to avoid my father when he came home from work. She knew by the time my father got home that he had already started drinking before coming home and he would get into an argument with mother; then he would start calling Terri some real nasty names.

I guessed that was one of his ways of hurting my mother because he never accepted Terri as his daughter and, at the same time, I was always being told I was the apple of his eye. This also started to put a wedge between my sister and me.

My mother would cook dinner for Terri and I before my father came home. Then she would cook for him when he got home if the arguments between them were not out of hand yet. I can recall one time when the argument between my mother and father got so out of hand, my father picked up and threw a porcelain ashtray that hit my mother in the upper part of her leg so hard she could barely walk the next day, not to mention how black and blue she was.

By 8:30 in the evening it was time for me to go to bed, at which point I never wanted to go to bed because I felt as long as I was up they would hold their fighting down. My mother and I shared the same bedroom so my father had his own room. In our bedroom mother and I had twin beds but as long as I can remember I was always too afraid to sleep by myself. Every night after mother came in the room I would crawl in bed with her.

By morning mother and I would get up to go downstairs to the kitchen only to find eggs and tomatoes smashed against the wall that my father had done the night before. This started to become an all the time thing. Mother would clean up the mess before my sister and father would come into the kitchen.

Normally, Terri came in first to catch a quick bite to eat or just to say good-bye before leaving to go to school. She wanted to avoid my father and she always made sure she was out of the house before he came downstairs.

By the time my mother and father were in the kitchen together there was a dead silence, which was normal for them because if they were not fighting they did not speak.

By the following year it was time for me to begin school and I was scared to death to be away from home. By the time I saw the school bus coming I would begin to cry and scream. My mother had to get one of the neighbor's boys who was a young teenager to sit next to me on the bus so that I would not try to get off. However, after awhile I finally got adjusted.

When I was seven years old my father had his first heart attack. The doctor said it was from my father's drinking almost a bottle of scotch and smoking two and a half packs of cigarettes a day. He also said this was something my father had to stop doing. The doctor also told my father he could not climb stairs any longer, causing my parents to sell the house and we moved into a ranch house in Port Jefferson Station. During this time I became a young teenager who realized that I wasn't happy because my parents were still fighting. Even though my father stopped drinking, my mother did not. During the week it wasn't too bad because both of my parents were working. My mother was a cashier for a supermarket and my father was driving a school bus. However, by the weekend, when they were both home, it got bad. During one Sunday afternoon, when mother was cooking our Sunday dinner, she and my father got into a fight in the kitchen and I heard the yelling from my room. I went to the kitchen and found my father with his fists balled up ready to punch my mother who, at this time, had a carving knife in her hand pointing it at my father. I got between them with my arms stretched out begging them to stop. They did stop but only for a little while then they were back to yelling at each other. By this time I didn't know what to do so I ran into my sister's room while she was out and called the police and told them what was happening. When they got there and told my parents they received a call from me about the fighting, my parents were both mad at me, but what was I suppose to do, watch them kill each other?

Needless to say they continued their constant fighting.

Chapter 2
MY ACCIDENT

AFTER STAYING in Port Jefferson station for approximately three years my family moved to East Setauket. While living there, my father had two more heart attacks and the doctor decided to put a pacemaker in his chest to keep him alive. Mother was still working the supermarket and my sister was also working.

I stayed in school up until the time of my accident on March 27, 1974. While I was at school, some of the girls and I decided, during break, to go outside to smoke some cigarettes. We were out in the parking lot of the school and while I was sitting on the hood of one of the girl's car she started the engine. I guess it was like a dare to see if I would jump off, but I didn't. After that she put the car into gear while I was still sitting on it and the car started to move. As we were going through the parking lot the car started over a speed bump and I fell off hitting my head on the pavement. While being unconscious I was told the girls ran for the nurse and by the time she got to me there was blood pouring out from my left ear.

Someone called for an ambulance and my parents who were at home and only five minutes from school. When my parents got there I was still bleeding, unconscious and throwing up what looked like black liquid, which we found out later was from a Pepsi I had drank earlier. After being in the emergency room for hours my parents were told that I had a fractured skull but that I should be all right when I regained consciousness. Well, after a week and a half to two weeks, I was still in a coma.

My parents received a phone call from the hospital at 11:00 pm from my doctor telling them to get to the hospital right away because he had found a blood clot on my brain and that I only had an hour to live if I was not operated on right away. My parents signed the consent papers for surgery and I was also given my last rites. After two hours the operation was over. The doctor came out of the operating room and when asked by my parents if I was going to be all right he told them that he could not give them an answer at that time. My father had to be sedated during the operation because he was showing signs of another heart attack. The doctor told my parents the only thing to do was to go home now and wait to see what happens.

The next day I regained consciousness realizing that I had to go to the bathroom. I looked around and saw all these IVs in me; some were clear liquids, another one was blood. I also found a tube stuck inside of me, and not knowing what it was there for I decided to pull out the tube and all the IVs. I got out of bed to go to the bathroom. While I was in the bathroom my parents had come to see me and when they walked into my room I was nowhere to be found, so of course they thought the worst. They went back to the nurse's station to ask what happened and a nurse told them I was there just a few minutes ago and that she had no idea where I was.

My parents and several nurses came back into my room finding my hospital gown on the floor. Then all of sudden the nurse opened the bathroom door and there I was, sitting on the toilet stark naked, wondering why was this nurse coming into the bathroom. I didn't know that the tube that was in me was for going to the bathroom. I guess this was the first time I ever saw my parents happy and mad at me at the same time.

I guess they knew, after seeing me up from bed the day after surgery that I was going to be all right. I had to stay in the hospital for a couple more weeks and during that time my family was bringing me newspaper clippings that told of my accident because I had no memory of it and as of today, I still don't remember the incident.

I remember the day I was released from the hospital, I didn't know where I lived and some other things I couldn't recall but the doctor said it was normal to lose my memory and he hoped things would come back to me in time. He also told me I would have to come back to the hospital in a couple of months after the swelling went down on my head to have a plate put in because I was missing a part of my skull.

After going home my mother bought me a wig because all of my hair had been shaved off for the surgery and I was too embarrassed to be seen by anyone. The teachers I had that year came to my house each week to help me finish that year in school which wasn't easy because I couldn't remember anything from before the accident, however, by some miracle I passed.

Some of my friends from school would stop by from time to time. At first I felt like I was on display for them to stare at and see what I looked like after the rumors went around the school that I was going to be a vegetable for the rest of my life. Then there was a rumor that I was dead. I guess I showed them, huh!

After a few months passed I went back to the hospital to have the plate put in. At this time, my father was in the hospital after having had another small heart attack. We were both on the same floor and my father came into my room the night before my surgery to tell me he loved me and that everything would be all right.

He promised me that he would be waiting on me to come back from surgery. The next day while I was being wheeled down to the operating room my father held my hand all the way to the elevator gave me a kiss and told me to hurry back. I told my father that I loved him and not to let anyone give up my bed because I was coming right back. He said OK with tears in his eyes.

I made it through the surgery and then after waking up in the recovery room I was bought back to my hospital room. I saw my father standing in the hallway outside of my room where he had to wait until the nurses got me back into bed. After they finished my father came in and we talked just for a few minutes until I fell back to sleep.

The next day my father was released from the hospital and a few days later I went home also. A few weeks went by then something strange started to happen to me. I started feeling a lot of pain in my head and it wasn't like a normal headache. It felt more like lightening bolts shooting through my head. I would start to cry and after it was over I couldn't remember what had happened and I was feeling totally drained of energy.

My parents took me back to the doctor and were told I was having an epileptic seizure and I would probably have them the rest of my life. The only thing to do was to put me on medicine for the seizures but that it would not mean that I wouldn't have more seizures. Here it is years later and I still take my medication every day but I still have occasional seizures when I get upset.

Chapter 3
THEE LOSS OF MY FATHER

I'LL NEVER forget the day I went to take my road test for my driver's license. I was so upset when I got home thinking I didn't pass that I had another seizure. After it was over my mother told me to stay in bed and rest, that she had to go on to work. My father told her that he was not feeling well that day and my mother asked him if he wanted her to stay home. Father said no, go ahead to work so she did. I fell back to sleep for a couple of hours and then one of my girlfriends stopped by just for a little while, long enough to talk about boys and then laugh about a few of them. During this time my father was in the bathroom so when my friend was leaving I walked out with her to get the mail. After we said goodby to one another I went back into the house and knocked on the bathroom door to tell my father he had gotten some mail but he didn't answer me. So I knocked again and still no answer. I went to open the door a little but it felt like there was something against it. I ran out of the house and across the street to our neighbor's house, knowing that Bob use to be a policeman. I told him that my father was in the bathroom and wouldn't answer me and also that it felt like there was something against the door

Bob ran back to my house with me and he went into the bathroom through another door that was off from another room. When he came back out he told me my father was on the floor and he was dead. I screamed "NO" and ran to the phone and called for an ambulance, and then I called my mother at work. I don't remember what I said to her but I do remember hearing the phone drop.

After a few minutes the ambulance showed up with two policemen. My mother came home with a couple of her friends from work, one of them driving my mother's car. The same doctor my father and I had came to the house a little later. I guess it was to pronounce my father dead. After that he wrote me a prescription for Valium on top of the other medicine I was taking for seizures.

Chapter 4
RUNNING AWAY

After my father passed away, I decided to quit school and get a job. I started working at a fast food restaurant called Jack in the Box. Eventually, after a few months I was fired after being accused of stealing money, which I knew I didn't do but I got fired anyway. After that I just started hanging out at the mall with other kids around my age. I was feeling kind of lost not knowing what to do with my life.

After a few months my mother had a stroke and I felt like the whole world was coming down on my shoulders. First, losing my father and now wondering if my mother was going to die also. I just couldn't handle it any longer so I ran away. I left New York and ended up in Florida. When I got to Florida I called home and my mother answered the phone. I asked her how she was doing and she said fine and wanted to know where I was. I told her I was in Florida and had gotten married which was not true.

After a few months in Florida picking oranges for work, I got homesick and wanted to go back home I called my mother and told her that I wasn't married and wanted to come home but didn't have the money for a bus ticket. In a few days she sent me the money and then I was at the train station calling her to ask her to pick me up. Within fifteen minutes of arriving back in New York I saw my mother's car pulling up. Without shutting the car off, the driver's door flew open with my mother jumping out, running toward me with her arms open. As we were hugging one another, we both began to cry. Mother was saying, "please don't ever run away again" and I was promising her I wouldn't.

As we got back to the house my sister Terri was they're waiting for me. We gave each other a hug while Terri said "please don't do this again because I don't think mother could take it". Then Terri asked me if I remembered when she ran away to North Carolina making me realize it didn't get her anywhere and pointing out the fact it wouldn't get me anywhere either. When I was in Florida Terri had married a man I introduced her to and she was afraid to tell me thinking I would be jealous. I told her the fling I had with Chuck was over but to be careful because I didn't trust him and I knew he liked to drink alcohol and take a lot of pills. Mother said she felt my having a relationship with an older man meant I was looking for a father image; maybe she was right.

After I was home for a few days I got in touch with this girl I use to work with. She was a little older than me and I told her I felt like going out. She said she was planning on going to this bar she knew of and asked me if I wanted to go. I said sure but knowing I was only seventeen I asked if she thought I could get in. She said "no problem" and that she would pick me up at 8:30pm.

So, here we go, to the bar and me having no idea that I would run into other people I use to go to school with or meet other friends of theirs. I met a guy named John and I noticed that we were attracted to one another. He asked me out on a date the next night and I accepted. After a few dates we were known as a couple, what kids called "going together".

Chapter 5

THE VISIONS

A FEW MONTHS later John asked me to marry him and I said yes. We were married on December 7, 1975, in a little church I used to go to. After the wedding John and I lived with my mother for a while. One night, while John and I were asleep, I had a vision that something terrible had happened and it involved my sister. I remembered waking up and looking at the clock that said five minutes to four in the morning. The phone rang at four o'clock and it was my sister screaming to me (get mom and get here fast). I hung up the telephone, woke mother up, and said something has happened and we need to get to Terri's right away. Mother woke up a friend of the family's that had come for a visit and told me that since John and I were already dressed to go ahead to Terri's and that Gil and her would be right behind us. John and I flew down the highway getting pulled over for speeding. I jumped out of the car and told the policeman that I had just received a call from my sister and that something had happened and that if he wanted to give me a speeding ticket to follow me there because I couldn't wait around for one. He told me to go ahead and to be careful. I said I would and left. By the time I got to Terri's there were five police cars outside the apartment where my sister lived. John and I got out of the car and went towards here apartment door. At this time, one policeman stood at the door blocking anyone to go in, I saw my sister sitting on the couch with her hands over her face crying her eyes out. The policeman told me I couldn't go in and I told him that was my sister and he had better get out of the way.

When Terri heard my voice she got up from the couch heading towards me screaming my name and "help me, help me". I pushed the policeman's arm from across the door and Terri grabbed onto me. I was wearing a T-shirt with two sweatshirts and my sister's nails dug right through them to leave imprints in my back.

I kept asking her "What is wrong?". She finally told me Chuck had shot himself in the head while she was lying in bed and he was sitting on the bed. When he shot himself, his body fell over on her. By this time the detectives were asking her a lot of questions and mother showed up. I met her outside and told her what had happened. Mother and I went back in while John and Gil remained outside. Finally the police got done checking my sister's hands for gunpowder, and they removed the body. Sometime later the phone rang and I answered it to hear one of the detectives tell me they had to come back because they couldn't find the bullet. After they came back the bullet was found in the wall up above the closet, then the detectives asked if one of us would come to the morgue to identify the body. I could not understand the reason for this but mother said she would do it. When that was over we all went back to her house and that's when I told her about my vision.

Terri moved back to mother's house and John and I had rented an apartment in Rocky Point near his parent's home. While we were living in this apartment I had another vision, this time it was to do with John's family. It was later in the afternoon when I woke up from taking a nap. I told John to call his parents house just to see how they were doing. For some reason, after no answer for several hours I told John to drive over there and to see if anyone was home. I remember feeling very uneasy at the time so I told John I would wait at home. After about an hour John came home crying while he sat down at the kitchen table. He said his father killed himself by stabbing himself in the heart with a kitchen knife. John's father had been very depressed for a while from losing his job after working there for many years and he left a note, that was later found, saying he felt that his family would be better off without him.

Chapter 6

DIVORCING JOHN

After several more months, John being in-between jobs, we moved back in with my mother and sister. Mother decided to sell the house and we all moved into a condominium in Port Jefferson Station. While living there I ran into my old boss from Jack in the Box and he apologized for firing me as he had found out it was not me stealing the money, I told him I understood and accepted his apology.

One night, while mother had gone upstate to visit some friends, John had invited a friend of his over and the four of us including Terri sat out on the patio and listened to music. John and his friend were drinking beer while Terri and I drank Pepsi. I felt kind of funny about this friend and kept wondering why this guy was going inside the house so often to use the bathroom.

A few days after mother returned from her visit she was in her bedroom and I was in mine when I heard her scream that her rings had been stolen. As John and I looked around the house John noticed his watch was gone too. I turned to him and said, "so that's why your friend had to keep coming in to use the bathroom!". I told him to get up with his friend and tell him to give back the rings or I would call the police and he would lose his job in the bank where he was working. John told me the next day that his friend didn't have the rings or his watch. I told him I didn't believe that for one minute so I got into my car with John and drove to the bank. John stayed in the car while I went inside and told his friend that if the rings were not back by tomorrow I was going to press charges on him and I would also have him lose his job. The next day mother went to the mailbox and there were the rings inside a paper napkin. After that happened, something told me that John was in on it and that his watch was taken only to cover the plan.

After a few months mother realized the bills were getting too high at the condo, and we moved to a split-level house in Nesconset. The landlady lived upstairs and mother, Terri, John and I lived downstairs. The rent was cheaper and the bills were easier to pay. While we were there John and I started having our share of arguments. I guess part of it was from my lack of trust in him. Well John decided to buy a new car hoping to make things better between us. We didn't have any credit so my mother co-signed for a 1976 Grand Prix.

After driving the car off the lot I filled up the gas tank and drove home. John took the car to work the next day and by that afternoon I received call from the hospital telling me my husband had been in a car accident. Mother drove me to the hospital and there was John acting perfectly fine to me. I asked him what happened and he said that he went to pass a van and had a head-on crash with another car. He left out the part that he had quit his job that day and was out driving around and drinking beer. John was released from the hospital and mother took us over to the station that had towed the car. The car was totaled and we were left making payments on it.

About a week after the accident John got another job and we started to talk about starting a family. I told him in order to do this that I had to stop taking birth control pills and I thought we needed to put some money together and get out of the debt we were in. He thought I was right and decided to give it a little time. A few months later I caught John smoking pot in the bathroom and told him this was it, the marriage was over. So in 1977, John and I separated, he moved back in with his mother and I stayed with my mother.

Chapter 7
MY TRIP TO COLORADO

At the end of 1978 I received the money from the lawsuit my parents filed on my accident in 1974. With that money I bought a 1975 metallic navy blue Camero and in gold lettering I had Sweetheart written on it.

After the landlady started giving us a hard time about all of our cars being parked in her driveway, my mother decided it was time to move again. So we rented another condo in a town called Ridge. I liked moving there because most of my friends were close to Ridge.

One night when I drove over to Rocky Point to visit a friend of mine, I ran into John. We both said hello to one another, then he looked at my car and said, "I guess we could of made it huh?". I said "not in this lifetime, bye" and left. I didn't feel like we really had anything to talk about.

During 1979 I took a trip to Colorado to visit a friend of the family. I stayed with Eva for two weeks having a wonderful time. Eva lived in Denver and drove me through Boulder; it was so beautiful there and the people were very nice also. After my visit, Eva drove me to the airport to catch my plane. I knew she had to be on her way work so I told her to go ahead to work and that I would be fine while I waited for my plane. We said our good-byes and she left. While I sat there waiting for the plane this very handsome man with blond hair and blue eyes came up to me and asked me for a light for his cigarette. As I handed him my lighter he asked me where I was headed. I told him New York and he then asked me if

I was traveling with anyone. I said no and then he asked, while I was waiting, could he sit down next to me. I said "of course". Here I was trying to play it cool while I was shaking all over inside. This man was gorgeous! As we talked and walked around the airport terminal he asked me if I had any plans coming back to Colorado. All I could think to say was, "you never know, I might".

When it was time to get on the plane, he asked for my phone number and after I gave it to him he leaned over and kissed me. I felt like I never wanted that kiss to stop. As we said our good-byes he told me he would be calling me. As I boarded the plane part of me wanted to turn around, but I held my cool and I kept on going. During the flight I stared out the window asking myself how could I have feelings for this man that I didn't even know.

After a few months back in New York, Jim called from Colorado and asked me if I would like to come back to Colorado for a visit with him. I told him I would and a week later I was on a plane back to Colorado. He met me at the airport and as we were leaving he told me he was staying in a mobile home and it wasn't much of a place. Boy he wasn't kidding. The mobile home was old and there was no electricity. As we talked and lit candles I asked myself what have you gotten yourself into this time. The next day Jim said he wanted to visit some friends of his that had a cabin up in the mountains and that we could stay there for a few days. I said "that sounds good to me" knowing it couldn't be any worse then where we were.

As we got to the cabin this couple came out and greeted us. The cabin was beautiful. We stayed there for two days and by this time I told Jim it was time for me to get back to New York. It wasn't really time to leave because I had my flight planned for a week but by this time I knew no matter how good looking he was, he was a bum living from place to place so all the butterflies in my stomach were gone and so was I.

Chapter 8
MEETING PAUL

When I got back to New York I realized I didn't like sitting around the house so I decided to start hanging out in the bars. I felt there would always be someone there to meet and hang out with. I learned how to shoot pool and became pretty good at it.

In November of 1980, while I was in one of the local bars, this man by the name of Paul came in and sat down next to me. After awhile he asked me if I would like to shoot a game of pool, I won the game and he asked to buy me a drink. We talked for a while and, before leaving, he asked if I would be there the next night. I answered "yes".

The next night Paul came in and we hung out together. During the night, as we talked, he told me he was married but he was planning on leaving his wife even through she was seven months pregnant with his second child. He was also telling me that he had no intentions of marrying her when he did but he got her pregnant and felt he had no choice. He kept on telling me how unhappy he was. I noticed he had drank a lot of beer that night and I thought he might have not realized what he was talking about so I really didn't pay too much attention to what he was saying.

As Thanksgiving came around I invited Paul over for the holiday dinner with my mother, sister and myself. My sister was being very rude like she always was whenever I had anyone over. My mother was happy to have her daughters that didn't get along with her on the holiday and Paul was fine as long as he had his beer.

Later that day while talking with my mother, I mentioned to her that Paul was moving in with us. I knew she didn't like the idea too much but to keep peace with me she said it was OK.

During the first week Paul was there I was driving him to work early one morning and skidded on a patch of ice ending up under a 1958 Mercury that was in front of me I knocked off her rear bumper and the front end of my Camero was gone. Several weeks later my sister was acting really nasty to everyone because of Paul being there so my mother came to me and said that Paul would have to leave. So, when Paul left, I left also.

We stayed at a motel for about two months and during that time Paul got up with a friend of his and bought his Dodge Charger that had already been hit with a snow plow. The driver's side of the car was smashed in but it got us around.

We finally found an apartment to rent, which was the downstairs of a house. While we were living there Paul seemed to get drunk more often and when he was drunk he didn't seem to be the nice guy I knew.

One day, while Paul was driving the car down the highway with no driver's license, he had already been drinking. I asked him if he would let me drive. Well, with one hand on the steering wheel he said if I didn't like driving with him then I could get out. He reached over and opened the door on my side and tried to push me out of the car while it was moving. He then grabbed my left hand and bent it backwards until I started screaming "stop it, your hurting me". He let go of my hand and then slapped me in the face a few times. He kept screaming at me until he dropped me off at his parent's house. He left again and his mother took me to the hospital to have my finger x-rayed because I couldn't hold it up. My pinkie finger was broken in three places.

One night, after Paul had too much to drink, he started getting real nasty with me by calling me some awful names. He then grabbed the keys to the 1969 white Ford pickup we had and was leaving the house. Knowing that he didn't have a driver's license since he was sixteen years old I stood in front of him and reminded him of that fact and offered to drive him where he wanted to go. Well, he back handed me across the face and told me to get the hell out of his way. This became a routine for Paul on Friday and Saturday nights, start a fight with me, get mad and then take the truck and go out.

Chapter 9

OVER THE BRIDGE

ONE TIME I got a call at 2:00 am from a man I didn't know. He told me your husband is all right and he is on his way home. Then the man hung up. About a half hour later Paul called and said if the police come by don't tell them he was driving the truck. I asked him what was going on and he said just do as I say and I'll tell you all about it when I get home. Approximately five minutes after getting off the phone with Paul the police were knocking at the door. They asked if I own a 1969 white Ford pickup truck and I told them yes. Then they asked me if I knew a Paul. I answered yes, that I knew him but my truck was parked outside the apartment and that when I went to bed someone must have stolen it. They then told me the truck was hanging off Smith's Point Bridge. All I could say was "WHAT". After the police left I was wondering if this was a nightmare or was it really happening. I went upstairs to the people who were living above us and explained what had happened and asked them if they would drive me down to the bridge.

After we got there I saw the truck with the left front tire hanging off the bridge with the truck pointed in the wrong direction. I opened the passenger side door and saw all the 8-track tapes and Paul's hat. Not knowing what to think I just went back to the apartment wondering if Paul was hurt. About an hour later Paul walked in laughing and drunk like nothing had happened. I knew there was no point trying to get him to explain so I decided to let it go until the next day when he sobered up. At least I knew he wasn't hurt. The next day he told me the bridge had an ice patch on it and he lost control.

We then went to the station where the truck had been towed and saw the front end was really messed up but Paul said he would fix it. During the next few weeks Paul got another body for the truck but it was taking time to replace it and during that time I guess feeling under pressure he kept on getting drunk.

One morning we got up and I asked him, like always, if he would like some breakfast. He got real nasty with me saying hell no and grabbed a beer for breakfast instead. After seeing him drink one after the other, I asked him "why are you doing this?". He got up from the chair and hit me so hard, in the face, I fell into the wall and you could see my body imprint in the wall after it cracked. The whole side of my body was black and blue for about a week.

Not too long after that the landlord came in because we were having water trouble and saw the big hole in the wall. Needless to say we were kicked out. We moved in with Paul's parents, which worked out because that was where the truck was and they also offered to let me use their cars whenever I needed go somewhere.

Paul's parents were very sweet people and treated me like one of the family even though I was not married to Paul. They were not happy with him leaving his wife and two children. I remember Paul's father sitting down at the table with me one night and telling me he felt I was making a big mistake getting involved with his son. He also told me that I had the right to know that a few years before he had to throw Paul out of the house because he kept on coming in drunk and he and Paul would start fighting which usually ended up physical and that would get his little sister very upset and that they could not have that in their home. Altogether there were four boys and one girl, Paul was the oldest.

Chapter 10

THE AX HANDLE

Finally, the truck was fixed and by December of 1980, four days before Christmas, Paul and I moved to Sneed's Ferry, NC. Paul was clamming for a living and was told that North Carolina was the place to go to catch clams.

By May of 1981, just after being in North Carolina for a few months, I got pregnant after running out of birth control pills. When I told Paul I was pregnant he told me that I better take care of it by getting an abortion or he would take care of it for me because he did not want any more children.

I couldn't believe he said that to me. I never felt so alone in my life. But in my heart I knew that it would be the best thing because I didn't want my baby to grow up in a home with their father being drunk all the time. I remembered what it felt like when I was growing up and both of my parents were drinking all the time.

So, I got an abortion before Paul had the chance to punch me in the stomach so I would miscarry.

During this time I started realizing how much I was afraid of Paul and how much control he had over me. As long as I agreed to whatever he said then I figured there wouldn't be any fights. As time went on and Paul got drunk and wanted to make love to me, I hated it. I couldn't stand it when he came on to me and tried to have sex with me but would fall asleep on me instead.

In 1982 I got a job working at this hamburger/game room joint that had pool tables and served beer. Paul liked to come in there after getting off the boat. He would drink beer, shoot pool and keep an eye on me. This went on for a couple of months and the more he came in, he would make me feel uncomfortable because he would get drunk and start making a scene. So I quit working there. A month later I started working out on the boat with Paul and I had to make sure I was doing every thing right because if I didn't he would yell at me like a dog. I worked with Paul until 1983 and that's when I started bartending at a bar down on Topsail Island.

Working there was not an easy thing to do because I could have a full bar and when the boss came in everyone would leave because he always came in drunk and was very rude to the people in there. I can recall one night when the bar was at its fullest and I tripped over some chairs while I was cleaning off the tables. It felt like something had ripped something inside of my leg. I told my boss that I had to leave and go to the hospital because I couldn't stand on it but he wanted me to sit on a bar stool with my leg

Inside of the cooler and hand out beers while he runs the cash register. I tried to do that but within 15 minutes my leg got so swollen I had to ask a friend of mine to drive me home so I could get Paul and go to the hospital. Well by the time we got to my house Paul was passed out drunk and had a heck of a time trying to wake him. After he woke up he cussed me out. I told him I was sorry to have to wake him up but that I needed help. At that point I didn't know what hurt worse, my leg or my feelings.

After waiting in the emergency room for what seemed like hours, the doctor saw me and told me I had torn the ligaments in my leg and had to walk on crutches for about two weeks. After that I never went back to work for that man again.

But, of course, with me not working and being around the house more it seemed to be one argument after the other with Paul. No matter how much I tried to please him by having clean clothes for him to wear, hot meals, and a clean house, it still wasn't good enough for him.

One night when he was drunk and calling me every name in the book, I decided I'd had enough and started yelling back at him. He grabbed hold of me by the neck with one hand while my back was up against the wall and with the other hand he was slapping me back and forth across the face. I was finally able to break away from him and ran out of the front door and over to the neighbor's house and called the police. While my neighbors and I waited outside their front door for the police to arrive, Paul came around the other side of their trailer with an ax handle in his hand and grabbed me again. The last thing I remember was being hit over the head with the ax handle. When I woke up I was lying on the ground with my right arm up under me and I asked the woman who was kneeling over me where my teeth were. She lifted my top lip and said, "your teeth are there but you probably can't feel them because your mouth is cut open". When the people from the ambulance went to lift me up that's when I realized I couldn't move my arm. When I got to the hospital my arm was x-rayed and the doctor was amazed it wasn't broken even though I had two black eyes, a split lip and black and blue marks around my neck, down both arms and legs, my chest, my back and a knot on the back of my head the size of a baseball. I guess I was lucky he didn't hit me where the plate was in my head.

The next morning I crawled out of bed after being awake most of the night because every time I heard a twig fall from a tree or a leaf fall on the ground, I thought Paul was back to get me again, even though I knew he was in jail.

I got into a hot tub of water that morning trying to get some of the soreness out of my body. After I got out from taking my bath the phone rang and it was Paul. He told me how sorry he was and asked me to please drop the charges. I told him I would only drop the charges under one condition and that would be for him to move out. He said OK. I then got dressed, putting on a long sleeve turtle neck sweater, jeans and my sunglasses and went to the jail and dropped the charges. He came back to the house with me, without saying a word in the car, got his things and left.

Chapter 11
SMASHING UP THE VAN

After about a week after Paul was gone, I got another job bartending down at the pier, which was only about 5 minutes from my house. A lot of local boys had heard that Paul and I broke up and would come in the bar and make passes at me. Well that news had gotten back to Paul and the next thing I knew he was coming into the bar. Instead of looking for a fight he was being very nice to me, telling me how sorry he was for what had happened. After believing him, he moved back in with me. Paul cut down on his drinking and we were getting along better than we ever had before.

Then one afternoon Paul came home early from work. He was drunk and looking mean. I asked him what was wrong. He looked at me with a dead stare in his eyes and said "what do you think is wrong bitch, how would you feel if you only caught one bag of clams". I told him that it was Ok because every day can't be a good day. Well he started yelling and I knew what this was going to lead up to, so I just let him keep yelling and didn't say a word because I remembered the last time I said something and he beat the heck out of me for it. I thought if he kept on drinking he would pass out and I would have a quiet night, but boy was I wrong.

He kept on drinking all right and things were getting worse. He was still yelling but by now it wasn't about his day not going right, it was about me. He told me how ugly and how fat I was and how no other man would want me and if I didn't like being with him then I could leave because he wasn't going anywhere.

I told him I was sorry that he felt that way about me and I wanted to stay there because I had no where else to go. By that time he grabbed me and threw me out the door screaming get out and don't you dare try to take the van. I walked into town in the dark and got to a pay phone and called a friend of mine and asked her if I could stay over for the night after I explained what had happened. She said sure and to stay where I was and she and her husband would come and get me.

The next morning I figured it would be safe to go back to my house because Paul would be sober. Well when I got there, Paul was gone and the windshield on the van had been smashed in. I said to myself that Paul can't keep on doing this and getting away with it, so I called the police to report what he did and told them I wanted to press charges.

They told me in order to do this I would have to come to the jail. So I got into the van, tried to start it but it would not start. I picked up the motor cover and found two hoses that had been cut and some wires that had been pulled out. I then called another friend of mine that knew some things about cars and told her what was going on. I asked her if she could help me. She came over and was able to put the wires back together and replaced the hoses. I finally got the van started and went to press charges.

Paul got himself out of jail the next day and was ordered to pay for the damage which came to $700.00. He didn't have that kind of money so he called his parents and got it. I got the windshield fixed and was able to keep my job bartending while Paul was staying at some friends.

After a few weeks the motor in the van blew up. I got in touch with Paul and told him what had happened and asked him which place he felt would be the best one to go and find a motor. He suggested a place and told me to call him after I went there.

I called Paul back the next day and told him they had a motor, which had been sitting outside, and the price they wanted. He said that they were crazy asking that price and for me to hold tight, that he would get me a motor. By the time I got off the phone with Paul, I sat there in a daze, wondering why did Paul want to help me after acting like he hated me.

After a few days Paul got a motor and told me that he was going to put it in because he did not want anyone else to mess with it. I thought this was really nice of him. He worked in the morning and part of the afternoon. After he got done selling his clams at the clam house he would then come over and work on the van. After a week and a half of this, I got a night off from work and asked Paul if he would like to stay for supper. He said that would be great. So, after it got dark and couldn't see anymore he came in and got washed up for supper.

During our meal we talked and he told me that he never meant to hurt me and that he loved me and was sorry for the things he did and promised never to hurt me again and asked me if we could get back together.

I told Paul that I loved him too but I couldn't take any more pain from him and I felt if he would stop drinking that things would work out between us. He told me that he was going to stop drinking because he wanted things to work out. He spent the night with me and by the next day he had his things moved back in. After a few more days the van was back on the road and things were going pretty well.

By fall of 1983 the clam digging was getting very hard for a lot of the guys because there were no clams to be found. So six of them, including Paul, traveled down the coast to Southport and tried digging for clams there. Well the clams were there and some of them traveled back and forth each day and the others rented a motel room.

By November of 1983 I noticed that Paul was drinking again. From what I could tell was that he had stayed away from drinking for almost a month but he was also staying down in Southport, sharing a motel room with some of the other guys who also drank. I really did not know if he stopped at all. He was making good money and seemed happy.

Chapter 12
PAUL'S PARENT'S VISIT

RIGHT BEFORE Christmas that year he told me that he had met this guy in Southport and the man offered to rent him a room in his home instead of Paul staying in a motel. It would be just a little while until Paul could find us our own place.

By March of 1984, we moved into this little old house on the outskirts of Southport. I got a job bartending at the bar Paul hung out in but that only lasted a couple of months because the owners of the bar couldn't afford to pay for help and decided that they would work at the bar. So after that I went back to clamming with Paul. By the middle of summer we had a large order for chowder clams and Paul and I went out early one morning while the tide was low. We got the clams the man had ordered and by this time the tide was coming in and Paul knew it would be over my head, so he said, "let's go in to the dock and unload the clams". Then he went back out and told me to go back to the house and pick him up at 5:00 pm. As we got to the dock I started helping Paul get the bags of clams to the car by throwing one of the bags of clams over my shoulder and hauling it down the pier to the car. We took the clams and sold them and then I dropped Paul back at the dock and I went home and took a nap. When I woke up and went to climb out of bed I felt this sharp pain shoot through my spine. By grabbing onto the nightstand and the wall I was finally able to get myself up, however, every time I took a step I felt this awful pulling pain in my right leg and sharp pain in my spine. I got out of the house and to the car, which seemed to take forever and drove down to the dock. I didn't get out of the car though which was not like me. When Paul got to the car I told him what had happened and also told him I thought I pulled a muscle in my back. He told me to slide over and he would drive and I was in so much pain I didn't argue with him about driving.

Since we were in town I told him to go ahead to the clam shop and sell his clams because there was no sense to take me all the way home and come all the way back again. Besides, I would feel better after I took a hot bath.

When we got to the house that's exactly what I did and when I got out of the tub I felt no relief. Paul said he felt I should go to the hospital and get it checked out and I agreed with him.

After I was at the hospital for a while I was told I had a slipped disc and the doctor put two needles in my spine. One of them was to reduce the swelling and the other one was for pain. He then told me that I would have to be off my feet and lay on ice for two weeks, while I took the medicine he gave me. I did what the doctor told me but I sure didn't like it. After that I was back up bouncing around again.

Approximately two weeks after I recovered, Paul's parents came down for a short visit while they were on their way to Florida. They came down in their camper, which was really nice. While they were here Paul's father decided he wanted to wash the camper and I wanted to help, so I took a bucket of soapy water, along with the hose, and climbed up the side so I could wash the top. After we got done the camper looked brand new. That night we decided to eat supper in the camper which was fun. During our meal the four of us sat around and talked, Paul talked about his day at work and how the clams were starting to be hard to find. Paul's father mentioned how beautiful the camper looked after he and I got done washing it and also told Paul that I was up on the top of it. Paul looked at me and said, "I guess she didn't tell you that she just recovered from a slipped disc". Paul's father's mouth just dropped opened and I came back with saying, "that was then and this is now and I'm feeling great".

It was starting to get late and the next day Paul's father planned to go clamming with Paul and his mother and I would go shopping. We said our good nights and Paul and I went back to our house. When we got in the house I told Paul that I wasn't going to let his father climb on top of the camper because he wasn't young any more and not to be mad at me for doing it.

The next morning Paul and his father went to work and his mother and I went shopping. When we got back we sat around and talked. His mother told me she knew that Paul wasn't easy to live with and she also knew he had a drinking problem. She hoped that Paul would stop his drinking and get his act together like his father did. I never knew that Paul's father use to get drunk. As I listened to her talk, I kept saying to myself "if you only knew the rest" but I didn't say anything because I knew how much she loved him and didn't want to hurt her by telling her how violent Paul got when he was drunk.

The next day Paul's parents left for Florida for a few months and were planning to stop by again on their way back home. After they left I went back inside the house and started to cry because I had such a nice time while they were here and I was already missing them.

Chapter 13
MY LEGS COLLAPSE

THE NEXT morning after I got up I noticed a red mark on the back of my lower leg about the size of a quarter. I didn't really pay too much attention to it until a few days later when that little red mark got a lot bigger. I thought it might have been a spider bite. A few more days past and this red mark had gotten very swollen and around my knee it was black and blue. I went to the doctor and he didn't know what it was. He sent me across the street to the hospital for some blood work. After about five to seven days I went to get out of bed and I fell to the floor, I could not use my legs anymore. They were both completely black and blue and swollen. It looked like someone had beaten both of my legs.

Paul got me in the car and rushed me to the hospital. They called my doctor and he told them to take some more blood and he would be right over. After he got there he told me that he honestly did not know what was wrong with me and he was doing a lot of blood work on me to try to find the answer. He gave me two different types of pills and told Paul to take me home and lay ice on my legs. I asked the doctor right then if I would walk again and he told me that he honestly did not know. I started to cry.

For days Paul would get up in the morning and put me on the couch along with bags of ice on my legs and leave for work. That was where I stayed until he got home. If I needed to go to the bathroom I would have to slide myself off the couch and onto the floor in a sitting position. My legs would be out and I had to push with my hands and drag my body to the bathroom and back to the couch.

One day as I was dragging myself back to the couch, I looked up while I was passing the kitchen and saw all the dishes piled up in the sink. I knew I couldn't stand up but I saw a bar stool that was in the kitchen and decided to pull it over to the sink. After I did that I used the bar stool and the counter top around the sink and pulled myself up on the stool. At that time I was able to get the dishes washed. While I was sitting there I noticed that the phone was in arms reach and decided to call my mother in New York and tell her what was going on. After I told her that I might end up in a wheelchair for the rest of my life, I started to cry. She asked me if I wanted her to come down? I told her "No, I was OK", which was a lie because I wasn't OK. I just didn't want her to see how drunk Paul got every night. I was ashamed.

After I got off the phone I crawled back down off the stool and over to the couch. After getting myself back on the couch with the bags of ice on my legs, I laid there and cried like a baby and then I started praying to God to please let me walk again.

After about two weeks it looked like the swelling was starting to go down and it wasn't as painful to touch my legs. In a few more days I started to be able to take a few steps like a baby. I looked over at Paul with tears running down my face and said, "look, I'm walking!". After a few more days I was walking around a little better, I was still very sore but was determined that I was going to get over this.

One night after Paul got in from work, I begged him to take me out somewhere because I had been laid up in the house for so long. He asked if I was sure I felt up to it and, of course, I said yes. So he took me over to a friend's home where we sat around and watched a movie. I had such a nice time being there and when the movie was over Paul said it was time to go because he had to get up in the morning. I stood up to leave and fell right back down again. Paul and his friend helped me to the car and on the way home Paul kept on saying that "I told you not to push it, but you don't listen to me". Of course, he was drunk again.

Eventually, I did recover but to this day the doctor I had still does not know what was wrong with me.

Chapter 14
HURRICANE DIANA

In September of that year we got hit by hurricane Diana. This was the first hurricane I had been through. As the reports came on TV and we saw that it was heading right for us, we took caution. We pulled the boat out of the water, brought it up to the house and tied it to two big pine tree with as much weight as we could afford to put in it. Paul wrapped the outside of house with plastic because he knew how drafty it was. We had flashlights, candles, batteries and bottled water.

By later afternoon on Tuesday, we sat on the porch and watched the pine trees that had to be about a hundred feet tall bend over with their tops brushing the ground.

Paul told me not to be upset because there was nothing to worry about. By about 9:00pm Paul was passed out drunk and I lay there listening to the wind howl and trees breaking. We had already lost electricity and I had the portable radio on, but it seemed every time I got a station to come in, that within five minutes the station was hit by lightning and turned to static.

I remember one station saying the winds were clocked up to 135 miles an hour. I heard the walls of the house creak and I know I felt a couple of times that "this was it". By the next morning when I looked outside I was waiting to see the boat in pieces and the van over on its side, but to my amazement, the van was fine and the boat, along with the trailer it sat on, with all of its weight had been pushed up along side of the trees it was tied to, but no damage.

When I saw the phone box outside, the cover was flapping in the wind with the wires exposed but we still had phone service. Paul wanted breakfast that morning and knew that the oven was electric so that was out. He took the motor cover off the top of his outboard motor and flipped it over and put some charcoal in it. We had an old barbeque rack and put that on the motor cover. After the coals were hot I fried up some eggs in a frying pan. By the afternoon the electricity was back on. I put the TV on and went into the other room. All of a sudden I heard the Emergency Broadcast System Alert and ran to the TV to hear that hurricane Diana had turned around while out to sea and was heading right back at us. I said, "Oh No, this couldn't be".

By Thursday, late afternoon, or early evening we got struck again and this time we got the eye of the hurricane, but for some reason it didn't seem to last as long as it did Tuesday. Again, we lost electricity after just having it turned back on. Paul got drunk and passed out and I laid awake all night listening to the wind and trees snapping like toothpicks.

The next morning, after the storm everything was the same except for a tree that had come down and just missed one of the corners of the house. We were lucky. We decided to go into town and when we pulled out onto our road we saw the main road in our neighborhood was gone. There were lakes on both sides of this road and one of the lakes got so filled with water that it ran over onto the road and into the lake on the other side and took the road with it. We turned around and took the back road into town and when we got there we saw two brick buildings lost their roofs completely.

As time passed, people were still recovering from hurricane Diana.

Chapter 15

TRYING AGAIN

Right before Christmas of 1984, Paul's parents stopped by again on their way back home. We talked about how much fun they had and what had happened since they left. This visit was a short one but, as always, I was glad to see them. Christmas had come and gone and so did the New Year.

By the beginning of March 1985, the landlady showed up told us she had sold the house and we would have to leave, which to me wasn't a big deal because I didn't really like the house anyway.

By the end of the month we moved into a big house that was right in town and right around the corner of our friend's home. The house was nice and it was clean and it even had a garage, which I knew was right up Paul's alley. Thinking things were getting better for us, Paul didn't seem happy about anything. He was getting drunk a lot more and had the "I don't care attitude". Trying to pull him out of his mood I decided to throw him a birthday party, which he didn't know about. After he got home from work that day I noticed he was getting drunk fast. I asked him if he could slow down a little because I had something in store for him. He starting cursing at me and wanted to know what I was up to. I told him that his friends were coming over for his birthday party. He grabbed a hold of me and threw me against the wall, screaming in my face that I had better call these people up and tell them the party was cancelled. I told Paul that wouldn't be a nice thing to do and he came back to me with "then go ahead and have the party but I won't be here". I said Ok, I'll tell everybody the party is off, just please calm down. He said "like hell I will" and as he was going out the door he ripped the screen door off. Later that night he came in and I was pretending I was asleep but that didn't stop him from yelling "get up bitch now". So I got up and listened to him while he screamed in my face some really awful things.

The next day Paul left and moved back to Sneads Ferry and to be honest, I was glad to see him gone. I felt that he had finally flipped out and went over the deep end.

After Paul was gone a week I decided I wanted to get out of the house for a while so I called up one of our friends and asked him what he was doing that evening and if he wasn't busy would he like to go out for a while. He said "sure" and 'I'll pick you up at 8:30 pm". We went out and had a few drinks at one of the bars on Oak Island. It was a nice evening, just feeling relaxed and not having to look over my shoulder every five minutes for Paul.

I got back to my house by 1:00 am and called it a night. As I started to get changed into my nightgown, the phone rang at 1:30 am. The woman on the phone told me she was calling from Onslow Memorial hospital and asked me if I knew Paul. I told her yes and asked her what had happened to Paul. She said she was a nurse from the hospital and they believe he had a stroke and wanted to know if I could come to the hospital. I told her "yes", but it would take me about two hours to get there. She said that would be fine, just please come. As I hung up the phone I caught myself staring at it wondering was this really happening? As soon as I realized it was happening I threw my clothes back on and jumped into the car. When I got the car started I saw the gas needle reading about 1/8 of a tank and I knew there were no gas stations open after 12:00 midnight in town. So I drove around the corner to my friend's house and explained the situation and asked if I could siphon some gas out of her truck so I could make it to Wilmington, and get gas there. Unfortunately she had about the same amount of gas that I did, so I told her I was just going as far as I could until I reached the first open gas station. As I was leaving I heard her say be careful. Boy she wasn't kidding, because the last thing I needed to happen was to run out of gas on a dark back road all by myself.

Needless to say, it felt like I held my breath until I got to the beginning of Wilmington and the first open station. When I pulled in and shut the car off I started to take my gas cap off. I could hear the suction of the gas fumes. I knew right then and there I had just made it. After I got my gas I was back on the road and I made it to the hospital in an hour and a half.

Chapter 16
PAUL HAS A CLOSE CALL

WHEN I got to the emergency room, the nurse told me that Paul wanted to see me but I was only allowed to stay a few minutes. She brought me into this room and there was Paul lying on this bed with all of these wires hooked up to him. He looked up at me with tears in his eyes and said, "I'm really glad you're here". The next thing I knew the machines he was hooked up to started to go crazy and the nurse told me I would have to leave the room because Paul needed to rest.

After sitting in the emergency room for five hours, Paul's doctor told me that he believed Paul had a slight stroke and he couldn't drink anymore because if he did it would more than likely bring on another one that could kill him. He gave Paul two different types of medicine, one was called Antibuse and that pill would make him sick if he drank any alcohol, and the other one was called Valium and it would keep him calmed down. The doctor then released Paul from the hospital. I didn't feel right to bring him back to our friends that he was staying with, at least not in the condition he was in, and I knew he needed someone to take care of him, so I brought him back with me to the house.

For days I noticed Paul was really out of it, the pills he took to keep him calmed down were knocking him out. After about a week or so Paul was acting more like himself, even though he wasn't drinking. He said he wanted to go back to Sneed's Ferry and back to work again, and while he was there he was going to find us a place to live.

I thought that this might be a dream come true. If Paul wasn't drinking any more, then maybe things would work out between us.

By the beginning of July I moved back to Sneed's Ferry into a trailer in a small trailer park right by the water. I was happy to be back and to see some old friends again. But not long after I had moved back, Paul was over taking the Valium so he went back to the doctor who told him he could die from drinking or taking too many valium and that he wasn't going to give him anymore Valium.

So by that afternoon Paul started drinking again it seemed like his attitude was worse now then before. Meanwhile I had met this couple that lived next door to us and Denise and I became the best of friends. When Paul and Denise's husband went to work, she and I hung out together.

On the other side of our trailer there was a young couple and the young man who lived there was a marine and he had a motorcycle, which he parked very close to our trailer by the bedroom. Every morning around 4:30 am we got woke up by him racing the motor on his bike and Paul was getting very upset by this. So the following Friday night, Paul was standing outside our trailer, very drunk and started to shoot off the gun he had bought and yelling he was going to shoot up the guy's motorcycle. The young fellow heard this and came outside with a shotgun and started firing off over towards our trailer.

I got scared and ran over to Denise's and called the police. They came and told both of them if one more shot was fired they would both be going to jail. I was really mad at Paul then because I felt if he wasn't so drunk that this could have been handled a lot differently.

By September of that year, 1985, Paul and I decided to buy a trailer that some friends of ours were selling. The trailer was old but in good shape and they were allowing us to make payments on it. We found a trailer park that had lots for rent and by the 1st of October we moved in. I was glad to get away from the neighbors Paul had trouble with but, at the same time, I knew I would miss not having Denise right next door, even though we were only about a 10 minute drive from one another.

Not long after we moved, I started bartending again at the same place I use to work on Topsail but a different owner had it now and he seemed like a really nice man. The second night I worked the boss asked me to be the manager there. He explained to me that I would be doing all the hiring and firing and along with everything else that came with that position.

So, after work that night I went home and told Paul I was the manager there, thinking he would be happy for me, but instead he acted like he didn't care. It seems as though we lived together with him doing his thing and me doing mine, with nothing in between.

Not long after I had started working there, Denise came by the house one morning and told me that she and her husband had broken up. After she told me this, I offered her a job bartending and she took it. It was great to be around my best friend again.

Chapter 17
MORE ABUSE

IN OCTOBER, Paul was arrested for drunken driving and driving without a license. The judge gave him three years but he stayed in prison about three months. Before he was released from prison on that charge, it was found out there was a warrant out on him from New York, so he got sent back to New York to face that charge. After his parents paid that fine Paul was released and came back to North Carolina. I hoped that he had settled down some from spending that time in prison. I was wrong! He got drunk the first night he was home.

By the beginning of 1986 Paul got into another argument with another neighbor. This time he fired the gun off in between the trailers. The landlord, who lived right down the street from the trailer park, was called, and by the time he got to the trailers he was very upset because this kind of thing did not go on in his trailer park. The landlord knew Paul drank all the time too and that night he had words with Paul but I didn't hear them because I was inside.

The landlord left and Paul came inside. I asked Paul right then and there what his problem was and who did he think he was firing off that gun again and then I asked him if he hadn't learned anything from the last time he did that. The next thing I knew was I got hit in the face, grabbed by my hair and pushed up against the wall. I screamed at him to just leave me alone but of course, he didn't listen. After he broke a few more things in the house by throwing them at me, he finally settled down and went to sleep.

The next morning the landlord and landlady came by and told Paul and myself, that Paul would have to leave, that he was no longer welcome there but I could stay if I wished to.

So that day Paul packed up his clothes and left for Pennsylvania where his parents lived. After I dropped him off on Highway 17, I felt such a relief.

After a few weeks Paul called and told me he was coming back. I told him that wouldn't be a good idea because I would then get kicked out of the trailer park. He said that he didn't care because he wasn't going to be run out his own home. I tried to talk him out of coming back but, by this point, I knew it was useless. I just wish I could of told him right then that I didn't want him to come back, but I knew if I had said that, he would come back just to beat the crap out of me.

That day, I sat in the living room by myself and kept asking myself when was this nightmare going to end. I was tired of Paul getting drunk and going into his rages and beating on me like a human punching bag and throwing and breaking things which was always something of mine that I cared about.

I was also ashamed to be seen with him in public because of him being drunk and the way he acted. He would never go anywhere without a beer in his hand and it didn't matter what time of the day it was. I was also ashamed to tell the truth about the black and blue marks on me when people asked, so I had to lied, telling people I fell down or walked into something.

I knew in my heart that people saw through my lies, so whom was I trying to kid, myself. I wanted a way out but I was living in fear of Paul and the fact that he knew he could controlled me.

By the next day, Paul was back at the house and within a couple of days I got a phone call from the landlady and she told me I had to move, so at the end of the month we moved the trailer to another park in Holly Ridge, which was the next town over.

I was still working at the same bar, when one night Paul came into the bar drunk and started to give me a hard time. He starting calling me some really nasty names in front of everyone and I took his beer from him and told him to get out, he was barred. He left and for the rest of the night and, while I was at work, I shook with fear of going home because I knew what he was going to do to me.

After I locked up and started to drive home, I thought that maybe Paul would be passed out I could go in without making any noise and sleep on the couch. As I pulled up to the trailer I saw a light on but I didn't see him moving around at all, so I said to myself "this is great, he's asleep". I unlocked the front door and opened it real quietly and stepped inside without seeing Paul until he grabbed me with one hand and with the other hand, he smashed the bar stool over my back. When he did that I hit the floor. Then he started kicking me. He then grabbed my shirt and pulled me to my feet and started hitting me in my face. I pushed him away from me and ran out the door and down the trailer park to the landlord's house and pounded on the door. He finally answered and I asked him if I could please call the police, which I did. They came to the house and took Paul out of the house, but instead of taking him to jail, they took him to his boat and told him to sleep on the boat for the night.

The next day I could hardly move but I went into work because I had no one to cover for me. Early that night my boss came in. He took one look at me and asked "what happened?". Again I had to lied and said I fell down my front steps. He said again, "I will ask you what happened?". and that's when the tears welled up in my eyes and I told him the truth.

My boss then told me he could see I was in a lot of pain and I could have the rest of the night off. I told him "thank you" and then I went home. Just after I was home for a little while the phone rang and it was Paul. Before he could get anything out of his mouth I told him I would bring him his clothes and whatever else belonged to him and drop it off wherever he wanted, but he was not coming back to the house and if he tried to I would have him arrested and he knew that he had pushed me to the point where I would.

He said OK, just put my clothes in my bag and bring them down to the boat. When I got to the dock, I saw him sitting on his boat drinking beer like always. I got out of the car and went down to the boat and asked him to get his clothes. He asked me if I was in a rush to take off or something. I turned around to him and said "I'm not in a rush or anything, I'm just in a lot of pain because of you and right now you're the last person I wanted to see". He asked me why I was walking funny. I pick up my shirt from the back so he could see from a distance how black and blue my back was. I then said to him "Now as you see I really don't think we have much to talk about!". I then got in the car and left.

Chapter 18
THE BURNING

THE NEXT day I went to the doctors and found out I had a chip in my main backbone now and that it could never heal. A few days later, Paul called again and asked me how I was feeling. I said "that's a stupid question to ask me after you put a chip in my backbone" and then I got "Oh baby, I am so sorry and I never meant to hurt you like that". All I could say to him was "then how did you mean to hurt me you jerk!". I told him point blank that I would never forgive him for doing this to me and I was not put on this earth for him to punch and kick me around any time he felt like it and I couldn't take it anymore. All he kept on saying was "baby, I'm so sorry". After that he said, "if I promise to cut down the drinking and not hurt you any more, could I come back".

I told Paul he could come back, but if he laid another hand on me that would be it. I reminded him I had a plate in my head and all it would take would be for me to be hit the wrong way on the side of my head and I would die. He knew every time he hit me I would cover my head for protection and never try to hit back.

Paul moved back in and things were going pretty well. In October of 1987, a friend of mine had some property that he had cleared and allowed us to move the trailer onto it. It was a beautiful piece of land, up in the woods, with just a few neighbors. I use to love to sit outside and see the dogwood trees in bloom and listen to the birds sing and watch the little squirrels run around.

I had a dog and two cats at the time and they would run around the yard chasing one another. It was really pretty there, and peaceful.

Not too long after we had moved, my boss had to let me go. He decided that he and his new wife would run the bar themselves. It was Ok with me because I wanted to start fixing up the yard.

The next month, which was November, Paul was back to drinking a lot and one night he asked me if I wanted to go out and shoot pool with him. I didn't really want to go because I never felt comfortable around Paul when he was drinking, but I knew if I didn't he would of taken the car and he still didn't have a license.

So I went and not long after we were there, while I was sitting at the bar and Paul was shooting pool, a man next to me started speaking to me. The next thing I knew, when the man got up to go to the men's room, Paul came up behind me and wanted to know where I knew that man from and what he wanted to talk to me about. I told Paul that I didn't know the man and he wasn't talking to me about anything important and to stop being so foolish because he was making an ass out of himself. He then said, "OK baby", gave me a kiss and went back to shooting pool. Dr. Jeckel and Mr. Hyde was a good way to describe Paul.

A little while later on, that same night, the owner of the bar came up to me and asked me if I wanted to bartend down the street. I told him yes and he asked me if I would like to work for him because he needed a good bartender. Paul was standing right next to me and said if I want to, that it would be up to me. I decided to take the job and the next day I started to work.

As the weeks went on and got closer to Christmas, Paul was drinking more and more. It seemed the closer we got to the holidays, the more depressed he got and the more argumentative he got also.

One night when I had the night off from work, Paul wanted to go up to the bar. He was already drunk and I felt that I had no choice but to go. While we were there, he tried to pick a fight with me and I just ignored him. After a little while he came up behind me and smacked me in the back of the head. I asked him what his problem was and at that point, he started to shove me and calling me a lot of names. He also accused me of cheating on him in front of all these people in the bar.

I grabbed my purse and ran outside of the bar. I got into the car and took off. I knew I couldn't go back into the bar that night and I also knew if I was home when Paul came in, that he would beat me. So I went home, just long enough to grab a couple of pieces of clothing and called my sister, who was living in Jacksonville now with my mother and told her what was going on. I asked her if I could come over and spend the night. Mother was in the hospital and I told my sister to promise me not to tell mother any of this because I did not want to upset her.

Chapter 19

THE SHOOTING

AFTER I spent the night with my sister, I went home the next day figuring Paul would be sobered up and calmed down from the night before. Boy was I wrong. He started swinging at me as soon as I got through the door, calling me a slut and wanting to know who I slept with last night. Through tears I told him I spent the night with my sister and if he didn't believe me he could call her. He told me that he didn't believe me and to get out. I told him I would get out because I couldn't take this anymore but before I left I wanted to get a few things.

When I walked into the bedroom to get my clothes they were gone. I asked Paul what he did with all of my clothes and shoes. He sat back with a smile on his face and said he had burned all of my things including the TV and the stereo too. I just stood there looking around for every thing I use to have and realizing it was all gone. My last words to him were "that's it". As I was running out the door he shot one of his guns off at me and said if I didn't want to die, then I better stop and get back in the trailer. I knew he would shoot me in a heartbeat so I went back in and soon as I got in he started to beat the hell out of me.

He first had me pinned with my back over the stove punching me in the face. That was the first and only time I believed I saw the devil in his eyes. I was able to get away from him as I got into the living room. I told him, as I was crying, that I didn't want to fight with him and that all I wanted to do was go take a bath. While I was sitting on the couch he took his .38-revolver handgun, which was completely loaded, with his finger on the trigger and put the gun up to my nose and told me that "you better stop crying bitch or I'll give you a reason to".

I stared at the barrel of the gun held up to my nose in fear knowing he would shoot me and not think anything about it because he had already shot one of my cats in the head and she walked around outside for three days with a bullet in her head before she died. Paul knew what an animal lover I was and that there was no reason for this except to hurt something I loved.

When I got up from the couch to go take a bath, he went into the bathroom before me and shot two bullets through the sliding bathtub doors and they went right through the outer trailer wall. Right then and there I knew this man was really starting to lose it and I didn't know what to do. The times I ran to get away from him he found me. All the times I called the Sheriff's Department and they had come out, the last time I called them I was told that the trailer was his residence and he had a right to be there, even though it was in my name. When I was on the phone with them telling them that he was going to kill me, they informed me that something would have to happen before they would come out to the place and I said "so, you're telling me that first he needs to kill me, then you want me to call back, right?".

This didn't make any sense to me. Should I go back home and just let him do what he's going to do? What choice did I have? I knew my dog was there and Paul had already tried to break the dog's ribs by continuing to kick the dog and when I saw him doing that I jumped on the dog and covered his body with mine and took the kicks instead of my dog getting them.

I kept asking myself how could his man be so cruel to my animals and to me? Thinking back off all the times this man would take my car at night and went out to get more drunk then he was before he left, and hearing the car pull up late at night I would pretend to be asleep so he wouldn't fight with me. There were times I really was asleep only to be woken up by a lamp being smashed over my head or him ripping my night gown off wanting to have sex. I couldn't stand having sex with him anymore, so I just laid there wanting him to get off me. I felt like I was living like a caged animal wanting to get out but couldn't! Remembering when he burned all of my things – he didn't even get my clothes out of the drawers that they were in, he just burned the drawers too. This man had complete control over me and I was scared to death not to look over shoulder at all times.

On Halloween in 1989, Paul called me from the clam house and told me to get my ass down there now, I knew he had already been drinking and this was only late morning. I went there and picked him up to bring him home. When we got back to the trailer I saw him drinking beer and also Jack Daniels and I knew when he drank the hard stuff that sooner or later he was going to hurt me. Out of nowhere he told me that I had twenty-four hours to sign everything over to him or I would be dead. He also said that he had a contract out on me and I knew right there that he was deadly serious. As he lay there on the couch I went to the bedroom, scared out of my mind because I didn't want to die. After sitting on my bed I knew if I didn't want to die that the only thing to do would be to kill him first before he killed me. I grabbed for his .38 handgun, loaded it and went back into the living room and shot one bullet into his head.

After that I freaked out not knowing what to do so I drove over to a friend's house and told him what I did and asked him if he would help me hide the body. He told me that I needed to call the police and turn myself in. I went back home and started to dig a hole in my front yard but after I started to do that I knew in my heart that it wasn't the right thing to do. I went into the house and called the police and told them what had happened. I was charged with first-degree murder but the charge dropped to second degree after many friends of mine came forward and told my court appointed lawyer what kind of person I had dealt with for the past eleven years.

After going in front of a judge, I served five and a half years in prison and was then released. Even though the bruises have gone away, the scars are still very deep! Even though it has been many years since his death, the month of May is not a good time for me to remember because Paul's birthday was on Memorial Day, May 31st and I can remember every year about two weeks before his birthday Paul would get drunk more so than usual, and pick an argument with me and that would give him a reason to beat on me.

Looking back I remember the second year we were together. I had a surprise birthday party for him and after the party was over and everyone left, Paul beat the crap out of me because I threw a party for him. I realized no matter how much you try to please a drunk, you can't. All these memories are ghosts from my past that still affect me today.

Because of what happened to me the bruises are gone but the pain and the scars are still very deep. I now have degenerative disc problems in my spine from all the beatings. I have to live with the pain every day of my life. I don't want to have surgery with screws put in my spine because there is a chance I could end up in a wheelchair. So, all I can do is take medication for it every day to try and ease the pain.

I hope this story I wrote about my life can help other people out there who are going through the same situation I went through. You need to learn that people were not put on this earth to be hit, kicked, punched or threatened and also know that once this happens, it is going to happen again and again if you don't get out.

Find a way out and don't look back.

The End

www.ingramcontent.com/pod-product-compliance
Lightning Source LLC
Chambersburg PA
CBHW031215090426
42736CB00009B/923